THE FOREIGNER'S SONG

Also by Pablo Medina

POETRY

Soledades (with photographs by Geandy Pavón)
The Island Kingdom
Calle Habana (with photographs by Carlos Ordóñez)
The Man Who Wrote on Water
Points of Balance / Puntos de apoyo
Puntos de apoyo
The Floating Island
Arching into the Afterlife
Pork Rind and Cuban Songs

FICTION

The Cuban Comedy
Cubop City Blues
The Cigar Roller
The Return of Felix Nogara
The Marks of Birth

MEMOIR

Exiled Memories: A Cuban Childhood

TRANSLATION

The Kingdom of This World by Alejo Carpentier
The Weight of the Island: Selected Poems of Virgilio Piñera
Poet in New York by Federico García Lorca (with Mark Statman)
Everyone Will Have to Listen by Tania Díaz Castro (with Carolina Hospital)

THE FOREIGNER'S SONG

NEW AND SELECTED POEMS

by

PABLO MEDINA

TIGER BARK PRESS ❋ ROCHESTER, NEW YORK ❋ 2020

Published by Tiger Bark Press,
202 Mildorf Ave., Rochester, NY 14609.

Tiger Bark Press books are published by Steven Huff,
and designed by Philip Memmer.

Cover art: Nightwalk by Greg Moschetti.
Author photo by Kassie Rubico.

ISBN-13: 978-1-7329012-7-8

Publication of this book made possible with public funds from the New York State Council on the Arts with the support of Governor Andrew M. Cuomo and the New York State Legislature.

Contents

THE MAN WHO WROTE ON WATER

POINTS OF BALANCE

THE FLOATING ISLAND

PORK RIND AND CUBAN SONGS

For John Skoyles

Moaneth away my mind's lust
That I fare forth, that I afar hence
Seek out a foreign fastness.

—"The Seafarer," translated from
the Anglo-Saxon by Ezra Pound

We bear within us the seeds of all the gods,
the gene of death and the gene of love.

—Gottfried Benn, "Can Be No Sorrow,"
translated from the German by Michael Hoffman

New Poems

THAT DREAM AGAIN

When God made the sea
he had with him a bucket of salt
and a bucket of sand.
He looked into the night
and fell into the space
he had shaped with his huge
nine-fingered hands.
I will not dream that this is happening.
I will turn into a bird and find
what I need to fill this place.
First he came upon the breath of angels
making bubbles on the beach.
Next he tried the hiccups of hermits.
They made the heavens sigh.
Then he mixed the urine of mongrels
with the spittle of saints.
Waves appeared and with them medusas
and fish of all kinds and ladies
in blue swimsuits and children splashing
and hairy men sitting under umbrellas.
The wind blew over the waves
and grew long dark tresses,
full breasts, beautiful glands.
God looked at what he made
and thought, *That is very good,*
and called it Island.

THE TRIALS OF PARADISE

How not to leave this island
of lizards and stone cushions?
How not to turn my back
on the sea urchin and the scorpion?

I'm going, as I said long ago,
to a field where the clouds are grazing
and the lilies hum an ancient tune of nebular origin.

On that field the ragged cows interpret
one another and swans waddle
wing-to-elbow with a lion
and an old dog frets
and bites its rump all day.
Such are the trials of paradise.

I promise to leave you all behind
dozing in your cave of shadows. The sun
is an owl's yawn and the stars
the roe of an occult bird.

Let me shake off the crud of the land,
let me sink in the waters that swallow snow
and make foam that no one understands.

SONG OF THE BROKEN ROAD

The road led to the swamp that swallows people.
I gave no thought to that, eager as I was to throw
my fishing line in the murk. I pulled up
Juan with his twitchy face, I pulled up Felipe
and the mule that kicked him on the head.
My grandmother sewed away. My mother
fed me corn, a little okra, octopus on rice.
I went to bed distraught and woke in a jumble
of telephone wires, calling here and there,
long distance and short. The road went straight
over mud and ended where the bombs burst
and the rockets glared. Then someone lit a pig
on fire and made it run through sugarcane.
The land sputtered and gurgled,
the sky flamed. Men screamed and died.
Not enough water in the world. Women
sewed and cooked. Out of the marsh came snakes,
alligators, bats, crabs, lizards, fish
that crawled and birds that swam. The warriors
cheered, my grandfather cried. Only the marsh
was still and the darkness lay on the water
and pressed down. Time before time in the depths,
creatures with three eyes and ten anuses, insects
with hands, occasional bubbles surfacing, reeds,
hyacinths, globs of growth. The fire was the devil's
business. That poor pig, those ladies in the house,
the frantic men. Where was I to go, back to the sleep
of skulls? Into the smoldering fields? Or follow

the road to the swamp? That's where the wise men
went to live with glow worms and minstrel fuel,
drink felicity from springs and dance a furtive fandango.

THE FRONTIERS OF SIGHT

Today I take on the soul of a bird,
a fish in the sea of the sky.
I find the solstice and the flag
of flowers that spill on the spiky
grass and look for you on the bed,
under the clothes you dropped
last night. The earth grows flatter
by the moment. Literature
is the light of the world, which you
no longer read or feel or dream.
You are the death of science
and its fountainhead.
You are the long, slow step
beyond the liminal sea.
I am the man without arms,
flesh of the stone,
a cosmic wind on the mountain,
kindling for the bushes of a covenant.
Sing me your monkey chant,
your song of the sphinx, lull me to sleep
like a biped on the frontiers of sight.

IN DEFENSE OF MELANCHOLY

At least once a week
I walk into the city of bricks
where the rubies grow

and the killers await
the coming of doves and cats.

I pass by the homes of butchers
and their knives sharpened by insomnia

to the river of black sails
and the torn-up sea and the teeth of dogs.

She waits for me in a narrow bed,
watching the rain
that gathers on the broken street

and the weak light of dusk
and the singing trees.

REASONS OF DARK

Living like I did,
eating what I could,
a can of beans, a loaf of bread,
I came to know
that hawks are hawks
out of hunger and the crickets
chirp in August out of lust.
I turn on a lamp
only for reasons of dark.
Midday and the moon
call me. Love, my love,
moves that way,
Chopin nocturne in the bayou
of my heart for you,
who makes me see
I'm no hunger monger.
The slow drip of the faucet
is a sign, a waking
with you and paint enough
to cover in white
the walls of my wanting.

THE ANDALUSIAN DOG FINDS ANSWERS

God likes to be played like a piano.
Dawn glows with sailors dancing in the eye of a storm
by the river of black water. These days
things make sense under the green and yellow
sky of Granada and I wear a tie as penance
for the sins of my navel. The saints of the north
and the saints of the south fly by dropping scorpions
down my neck and those women
with fire in their eyes drink melon juice and wink.
I play billiards on the other side of town,
thinking bone in and bone out is the legacy of canines.
The camouflage, the hunt, the war of ice and water.
God knows. He clinks all day and night.
Fly me to the moon. I'd rather be sleeping.
A slender, tender rain comes over Granada
and the storm passes and the city sighs.

NOW NIGHT

is the seed of exhaustion,
the folklore of the broken heart.
Here comes the guitar-made man.
Here comes a hare leaping over the grave,
a truth brigade, a long-lost relative
enforcing sleep with an air grenade,
love and its grinding gears,
hate and its lullaby.

Is a combine, a land mine, a centurion
barking orders to the Lady of the Lake
beside myth's abandoned fuselage—
the gorgon breath, the wailing nymphs,
fraudulent fruit groves
drowning in the foam of talk.

LOVE MACHINE

The rain today is falling
like fiddles, like fiery-cold fingers
that gather in puddles on the street.

Look, an overcoat leaps
over them. Inside is a man
whistling a tune of you.

Rain has not stopped him
or curdled his longing for speed
or made him sick with your absence.

The love machine is intact
amid the cars sluicing by.
Your dog doesn't bark in the rain.

He curls on the sofa where you read
and looks askance and waits.
Love is an ambulance yowling.

Love is the patient otherness
of the dog, the machine that rumbles
past the lights bearing corpses,

death and resurrection.
Your hands close the book,
water glosses the bare branches.

THE CONVERSATION

She wanted to escape her marriage,
he wanted to escape much more—
the island, the tropics, his troubles with the state.
In bed, where their best conversations took place,
he said, A young woman like you shouldn't be right
so often, and asked why she was with him.
Because you have shown me how to love.
How is that? Without hope and without promises.
No me mueve, mi Dios, para quererte,
el cielo que me tienes prometido,
he said, quoting the famous sonnet—
by Saint John, Santa Teresa? No matter.
Even with her he couldn't keep from showing off.
Poetry was his privilege and his gift.
Muéveme el verte en una cruz y escarnecido,
she said, impressing him more than he impressed her.
Who am I to you, he asked.
You are my lover and my beloved.
En la noche oscura del alma, he said.
And in the brief day of the body, she said,
sliding her hand to where his manhood lay.

THE MAN WITH THE MOTTLED FACE

The man with the mottled face
married the woman with the trembling breasts.
The cantaloupes chanted, the cabbages danced.
The bombs came raining down
on children and parapets alike.
She died among the ruins
looking up at the dusky sky.
Running away, he tripped and fell.
His nose shattered and his lips
bubbled with the fires of the heart.
He lost his lover and he lost his land.
His father was cannon fodder, his mother
a gunslinger in the pontifical wars.
Oh the short road of the lit cigarette,
the long road of waiting,
the tender glow of ascension.

As a child he entered the palace of dreams,
now he enters the capsule of time and grief
and chews the words of saints like a somnolent ox.
Saint of the split ecstasies,
saint of the thousand effigies of milk,
saint of the bullwhip of penitence.

Mottled faces of the world unite.
You have nothing to lose but your chains.
You have many moons to gain.

LOVE POEM WITH OCTOPUS

Doris and I came together
under a mango tree
kissing for the first time
in search of desire's deviation.
That year or the next
—who can remember?—
we were interlocking parts
of the human mechanism,
which has many entry ports
and no one to advise you.
Exhalation turned on a dance
of fluids and energy and, oh,
we palpated what we could,
imagined the rest and went home
singing a song of retention. God, I thought,
this is the pulse of the universe,
this is the mystery of the sea,
an octopus in the depths of an orifice
and fish hiding under the tentacles.

WHO WINS OUT

The poet makes things appear
out of thin air—coffee on the table,
table in the living room,
living room under the dome of the sky.
Look at the stars, how they multiply!
You, my rabbit, are back in the hat.
Magic taught me to make
crevices through which the truth
and the lie leak like rhetorical twins:
the one-eyed man and the wicked swan,
the laughing gull and the coconut.
You have to know them very well to tell
the difference between the mountains
and the church bells.
The sea flattens all forms and the words
to describe them. Far from the sea,
forms become their meaning—
nude woman in bed, man hoeing a field,
the deep sleep of a pregnant snake.
Who wins out in the end,
my mother telling me her dreams
or my father calibrating fantasies?

FURTIVE FANDANGO

People walk by me unaware.
A dog scratches her fleas and bites her side.
I dangle over the void
like a marionette in mid-strut.
Someone is pulling the strings,
someone goes home in a sangfroid
moment and curtsies before the king.
The king of what?
Of all the elements, especially the sticks
and stones that maul my bones.
What are you hiding?
I hide my lisp, my crisp consonants,
my glottal stops, my slurred vowels.
You're not from here. I'm not
from anywhere. *Then why howl?*
I am not howling. I'm gulping.
It's a trait of translation. My English
is not perfect. It's a steep downhill
to the music of the flatlands, identity in tatters.
My words are the ground and the wail of the sea.

EIGHT MEN ROWING

Eight men are rowing
the patriarch into a dream.
His tears feed the river
on which they row.
The river turns to city streets
bearing his name, wide with esplanades
and shade trees.

What happened here? he asks.
His teeth are in the drawer.
His pants are loose around the waist,
his eyes are brown dots
driving out the light.
He once thought he owned
the morning and the night and made
the afternoon weigh down
the steaming streets
where no one was allowed to walk
or talk except the eight men
who rowed him to the sea.

He sits on the beach
and lets the waves tickle his feet.
He wears a blue swimsuit. The sky
is like his belly but rounder.
He barks and there is no one
to listen or obey. The eight men

disappear. His children ride
their rocking horses to their own dreams,
his women turn to other gods
who smoke cigars and beat their chests
and drive fast cars in Miami without end.
The patriarch pants and sways
as if the wind were shaking him
to follow the caravan of years
under the sheets' white billow.

OLD LEGS OF MINE

Old legs of mine,
you're all I've got.
Old knees, thighs,
skin, you droop.
Down there
the fruit droop too.
Eyes, you squint.
Ears. What? Ears, I said.
Old navel, bushes, grass.
Hands like claws,
feet like slats.
The river old,
the water cold.
Old sleep, you're short,
old solitude, you're long.
I dig, I dig,
old smile that dazed the sun,
old heart that beat with joy.
I raised a boy
then I let him go.
Old names, you pass me by.
Old language, cat
in my throat,
My tears, you're stones,
old dawn, you crone
breaking on the shore.

AMERICAN FOOD

Once, when I lived in the Bronx, I saw
a yellow butterfly float over the train tracks
by the Hudson's spiky shore.
I went after it, jumping carefully over
the third rail, all the way
to the Harlem River, where the butterfly
disappeared into Manhattan.

It took me an hour to get home.
"You want a tunifish sandwich?"
the old lady who lived down the hall asked
and I said yes. Canned tuna I loved
and had plenty over the years,
as well as Chef Boyardee ravioli.
Now I am without tunifish or Boyardee
or bologna on white bread with mayo,
another delicacy of my youth.

"I'm dying," I told that sweet lady in a dream.
"What else is new?" she said and offered
a chopped liver sandwich. I bit into it
and gagged. I'd never tasted
the paste of inner organs.

Under the moon I went down to the street
and walked past Spuyten Duyvil and the Bronx
across the river to New Jersey, where I heard
a wailing, tender voice spitting out grape
after grape of purple angst.

American food makes sense
if sense is what you look for
and you're hungry from your travel
past the devil's spite and the tunifish,
the chopped liver and the butterfly.

MOON MONKEY

The sun is blasting through the window
in a fanfare of light and it (or he? or she?)
corrects my mood, infects me with hope
(hope mother of love and spring). Snow
has no dominion, having turned to gray
kernels in the corners of the parking lot,
winter's broken smile curling into nothingness.
A man wearing thick glasses looks up:
Ah, blue. Boo to the sordid, slapping wind.
He must be thinking of love—the sun
awakes in him a fantasy, having already
eaten his lunch—and maybe his wife, maybe
his lover. He sees a stranger take off
her coat. She's a monkey, hair on her chest
and a chummy smile. This happens
often on my block, beautiful women
turn into simians, men become paralyzed
by absolute imperatives. I wanted to say
when this poem began that I love you,
I wanted to undo years of reticence
under the moon when things begin to swarm
and the worms burrow out of the earth
and you're blinking on and off your desire.

SPRING BEGINS IN BLACKSTONE PARK

My friends the sparrows
return to my window
chirping with their quirky,
bulbous chests and their
tree to tree exertion.
No pasarán.
A lady in dark glasses passes.
A man repeals his private law
against the smile.
Wish the sun were stronger
but I'll take the balmy sky,
the promise of soft air
leading me outside. I
have no feel for the divine,
not now, when spring begins
in Blackstone Park.
No pasarán. War mongers:
go home. Deviants: trace belief
through a child's temple,
find grace in the street
cleaner eating a popsicle.
The park today is Eden,
and the fruit is fulsome
and sensational.

The Island Kingdom

2015

THE ISLAND KINGDOM

La maldita circunstancia del agua por todas partes. *
—Virgilio Piñera

I was born to an island,
the drum of the world,
where the saints pattered
and the demons danced.

I was born to the beat of her hide,
the violin of her vertigo, the laughter
at catastrophes of weather and heart,
wrapped in a bundle of propensity
as thunder rumbled and the rains came.

I could hear the thrumming
of the wind under her voice:
too much poetry, a deluge of it.

I was undone by her confines,
her opening and closing,
her fish swimming toward heaven.

She lay at the ready in a corner of the map
and left no trace that could not be wiped with a rag.
I wanted to stay forever next to her in bed,
but I knew she would serve any master.
Easily replaced, easily adopted,
she returned like the shadow of emblems
and the face of particulars—mother, father,
third cousin I saw washing between her legs.

At night the island lingered and danced
on the wall like a candle.
She didn't like fire
though she often filled with smoke.
Never dormant, never a dove
flying across blue skies,
sometimes lips half open and a snake
coiled on the rock of decorum.

She went by many names—
parasol, crocodile, scimitar, whore—
turning on herself, alone and inconstant,
ship sailing to the end of time.

* *The cursed condition of water on all sides.*

THE RIVER SAINT

River brought headless dolls,
two-legged stools, torn dresses,
beach balls, melon rinds,
the bones of cattle and pigs.
It brought many conundrums
about what a river is—tongue,
gullet, colon, liquid road.
River didn't clang or make song,
banks muffled by silt and sewage.
River brought wounds, river brought
time. River was one meandering vein,
mouth open to the stars.

Once I watched a body floating
like a ship sailing off
on a one-way voyage.
I went home with the news
and the men came running back.
The body was under the bridge
by then. The police arrived
and fished it out. They made
me turn away too late. The nose
and one eye were missing,
face a round sponge.
River brought a dream
and every night until we left
the face came up from the black
waters and lay next to me in bed,
wanting only the moon
and the comfort of memory.

TOWARD THE ISLAND

1.

Smell a forest, smell the sea
and the vulture
climbing the scales of the wind.

Smell a woman who loved you
between the sheets of abandon,
cloistered, beautiful, lethal as a blade.
Smell a lady with umbrella walking by.

2.

On the island the cold moon
mirrors an end-of-the-world snow,
so far from the womb,
so close to disdain.

Voice of no one follows you.
Island is a broke refrain:
wave and snow, wave and stain.

THE BLINDING LIGHT

Perch'i no spero di tornar giammai *
                                    —Cavalcanti

Huge eye of afternoon,
penetrable, empty,
the air empowered by matter,
the continent bereft
of latitude, repeating itself
like the rain that falls
or keeps from falling.
The rain that mimics mourning.

In the distance longing rings
and all is salt, moon,
circularity of absence.
All is island in the blinding light.

* *Because I do not hope ever to return.*

LADY BABEL

She came between two tongues,
she came between two suns,
then there was the neigh of horses.

She came between the light and the spiders,
the female eating the male,
the noise eating the laughter.

Inside her was the whisper of license,
a tender ice, a lead-pipe warmth,
a sphinx and a bone and white fences.

The words she left appeared:
the roots, the trees, the branches.
She fell in the abyss of the hens

and the river ran and my dreams kicked
and the apes had choices. A hummingbird
flew from flower to flower

sucking the nectar of longing.
The lady came up on the other shore,
lips painted with a thousand voices.

THE BLUE-FACED MAN

He thought it would be easy,
this falling in place in New Jersey, its rhetoric
of shore and clapboard, factory and lilac bush,
grave shadow and forest glen
where yesterday a deer defecated.
Who strikes back at manhood? (Shall a man
be held accountable for his fidelities?)

October rain again,
farmhouse left to rot in the outskirts
of Paterson, smear of tears on the face
of the girl on Bergenline.
What is the truth, the lie?
Who's driving the car?
The gods are tourniquets,
they stanch the flow,
like New Jersey but narrower.
Sleep Well Motel blinks on
and off. From the hill where he lives
the blue-faced man stares past the haze
at headlights moving through the black
mottled marshes of Hackensack.

SACRED HEART OF JESUS: 9/11/01

Sacred is the master plan with its emphasis
on tenderness and trembling. Gone arrogance,
gone reliance on blue certainties.

The visits of angels are confounding.
Sacred is the wreckage of memory.
The planes fly in and disappear as souls

disappear. No sanctity in clouds.
The chest is exposed,
the fire is alive in the heart of Jesus.
Bliss and death are one.

Across the street where the pigeons
coo and peck through trouble
the suited executive and the Chinese
delivery boy join the ruins and the crowds.

SAINT OF THE BUS TERMINAL

We heard the call of the bus terminal,
an inner hum like need. We craned,
we twisted, the need growing by the hour.
You and I together and the space between.
Then the archer's craft, long bow
slinging arrows into night.
We wanted to fill the space,
which became orifice, which became
tunnel, which became the strains
of a soft music once called love
but now called devolution.
We sacrificed our children
to the god of subterfuge, the goddess
of denial. We wanted penetration
into the country of peace.
Who would have thought opposition?
Thinking has no terminal
where the bus might dock. The entry,
the spiraling up, hell ascending,
hole after hole opening then shutting
behind us and the arrows missing
their mark, a city of smells, motors, moons.
We offered up a chalice hoping beyond
our senses for the light and the fire.
Upward we went and the light
dimmed and the fire died. Faces
fat and clammy or thin and arid,
the saint squatting in the corner
in love with our misery, the man running

to catch the bus to Bergen,
raincoat flailing, eyes melting.
We found God behind the glass doling out
tickets to Boston, Newark, Philadelphia,
his mother waiting by the gate to Providence.
Remember how we held each other
as we rose, how we wished
our tongues could loll, lick the archer's hand
and the mouth that swallowed us?

SAINT WALT

Lost today in the labyrinth of Brooklyn
I've come to stretches of lassitude
and aimlessness to find you,
old minotaur of sex and candles
and tourniquets and wrenches.
You, who walked through armed
with only your voice and your verve,
who left behind the aura of bravado
song and declension,
amigo, Whitman, Saint Walt,
master of machine and wheel, eater of bull
testicles and mockingbird tongues,
ubiquitous master, long-fingered handler
of the moon, slave of compassion. Wave after wave
crest in your tongue of wind and water
and your chest like a drum of sorrow.
Blackbirds of thought fly in your mind
darkening day. The streets of your Brooklyn
have taken up your manly smell,
your brash American inflection,
your roar of an animal in the wild,
your eye of an eagle hunting, your garbage trucks
and taxis, your vending machines, oil slicks,
sidewalks splotched with chewing gum,
your homeless, toothless, wireless love of all.
I saw you strolling down the avenue
and you were king and pauper, hater of knives
and whimpers, lusting after a young boy in makeup
and a rough man in leather and a woman

in high heels and fur coat, her lips pursed
and gleaming on your man-hard flesh. The night
was storm, ocean of clouds to the west, thunder
lighting the future at the end of self,
amigo of the lame and the blind, saint
of the wheelchair, of the brokenhearted,
of the two girls dancing the tango in a dim-lit bar.
Tell them there's no triumph or defeat,
no border between night and day,
no understanding who they are,
but a slow movement like their bodies move,
a slow tide like their bodies' tide,
a late spring bursting with ten thousand blooms.

ARRIVAL: MY FATHER'S DEATH

No breakage, no oasis card
or modifier garden, no nylon
adjudication engine, no, or cotton gin
reprieve. No old age,
no shadow cave, no licking
the feet of temperance.
Dumb spiral, moody river never,
no excess or deletion of fun,
no computation, cubicle, demerit,
typewriter canticle.
Trust is the rage of water,
sunlight aura on the palm tree.
No question, no answer,
no desert effervescence,
no cauterization sharpshooter.
A mackerel sea is the velvet place
of entry. Without that and every-
thing now on the surface, cow
concerto, no, no, eye Pantocrater,
hook, modernity, prison traveler
to the isle of ever, no, no,
household severance, gravity's grace,
expiration lotion.

THE PANTHER

Even as we speak, even as we breathe,
there is in the shadows a panther stalking
like a great clawing machine, its eyes miracle
entries to another universe where panthers
are masters and all is reflected
through their panther mind, we mere creatures
on the edge expecting any moment the leap,
the paw's swat, the elemental fangs
at the back of the neck breaking our spine,
making us flesh for its maw. Its yellow eyes
visualize what passes for the world,
what passes for a dream--the leaping doe,
the new born calf, the child getting water
at the river—real as the hunger that burns inside
the panther stomach. Then the nightmare
of the forest and the nightmare of the gunshots
and the leap over the rock into the foliage
and the sound of villagers screaming, hitting
the trees with sticks. Panther ears seek silence,
eyes darkness, mind a chain of thought—
pain, breath, water, sleep. Then the sound
of people again. The panther, now prey,
fights the instinct to attack, knowing
(this is all it knows) that to reveal itself is to die,
its will to live stronger than its will to kill.
Panther, panther, let the slaughter come,
let the truth be learned, let the bullet
blossom in you like the flower of forgetfulness.

THE RIVER OF PEACH TREES

Spring returns to the River of Peach Trees
Du Fu spoke about,
already old and sick, on his way south
after many years of exile.

My sail is a white cloud
surrounded by forests.
When I think of my old friends
I see featureless faces.
Sick with bitterness
I look north one last time.
No one remembers my tired verses.

LANDSCAPE

Rain, no one by the river, a voyage
through a dark wood where the naked
trees are groaning.

On the far shore someone
is playing the radio, someone is talking.
Light moves again through the trees and disperses,
spreads on the moss, then ascends.

The Man Who Wrote on Water

2011

MY MOTHER DREAMS ME

My mother dreams me and I wake.
She wakes. I dream

she is alive. She rises with the sun
as always when I sleep.

Her ashes mingle in my bed.
She seems to whisper to the wind.

My mother is awake, asleep, who knows?
She roams the sea. She spills

into the dark like salt. How is it
that she dreams, how is it that I wake?

My mother sings without remembering.
She is the edge of rest,

the glow of doom, the grapes
I ate the day she died.

NOT ALL OF ME

*Non omnis moriar, multaque pars
mei vitabit Libitinam.**
—Horace

23rd Street, early morning broken down
station wagon fender askew.

Rain about to fall, trash
spilling out of the wire baskets,

two men at the corner arguing baseball.
Upstairs I find a message

that I read and read again—
a salty grief coming through my skin—

last night's poison, last night's dream?
A poet friend died in his sleep,

a hurricane tore through the south.
Inside me an ocean is thickening.

Not all of me will die,
taste of the earth in my mouth.

* *Not everything will die, and a part of me
will live on in the grave.*

AT THE BLUE NOTE

Sometimes in the heat of the snow
you want to cry out

for pleasure or pain like a bell.
And you wind up holding each other,

listening to the in-between
despite the abyss at the edge of the table.

Hell, Mulgrew Miller plays like a big
bad spider, hands on fire, the piano

trembling like crystal,
the taste and smell of a forest under water.

The bartender made us a drink
with butterfly wings and electric wire.

Bitter cold outside, big silence,
a whale growing inside us.

THE DAYS OF GLORY

As a boy I dreamed of girls
dancing naked in their bedrooms.

Later I wanted to know how their nipples
tasted—marzipan, strawberry, chocolate fire?

Later still, I was slave to their shadows
and their soft ways and their sea moans

and the thicket of wildness under their skirts.
In the city now, tied to the mast of marriage,

I taste fresh hay, I taste a salty marl.
I see a woman crossing Fifth Avenue,

maculate, indelible, looking
very much like my mother.

The long neck of the avenue swallows
the days of glory, the days of desire.

THE FIRE EATERS OF MEXICO CITY

Under the light of the empire
the world is fleeing the moon and its amber.

Some invoke the need for peace.
Others fall asleep in alleyways.

The boys on the street chew like dogs
the last bones of their longing.

Against the ancient curse and claim of power?
Huddled in blue mounds, open to rapture.

Only a river washes out memory.
Only a labyrinth sings

to another labyrinth. At midnight
they call to each other, Who goes there?

The heart's land glows in the fire
and the children, no ocean, eating that fire.

THE MAN WHO WROTE ON WATER

How soft they are, the little words of your insides,
how they slip out and drop in the water,
sinking a few inches then floating to the surface
like the leaves the river takes down to the sea
where all words go, liberate themselves, become one.
Three years you sat at the river's edge. The moon came
with its orange face. The blue heron came, angular, indifferent,
and the great horned owl, spreading vast wings over the house,
and snow and solitude so deep your thoughts
froze where the river narrowed and looped and buckled
on itself. Lovers came, left behind books,
a photo or two, tiny candles in the dark fields that the wind
blew out before you found them. When the ice melted
more words appeared: magnolia, madreselva,
goldenrod, sumac, sinsonte. The surface
bubbled over rocks, the river flowed and you caught
minnows cupping your hands (as a boy
on the Río Quibú). The sun beat hard on your nape.
You went to your room and put the wounds on paper:
home, distancia, campana, aphasia. The dog ran
back and forth on the lawn searching for bones.
A plastic bucket in the corner full
of crumpled trash, dust balls, torn pantyhose,
the papers before you swallowing, thickening
like snow. Some days you'd hear a plane overhead;
most days it was silence and the river sighing.
You were writing the wrong words.
You were making meaning without sound. The river
flowed fast there after rain and the water churned language

into foam. You went inside to dim light and the page,
another winter hearing the ice groan,
the hoarfrost gather on the dogwood branches.
The landscape was in you, you in the landscape,
the flow of water to the sea always the same,
never the same, and when you left it was summer,
the history there already in the water
moving past you to its rendering.

SAINT OF THE FOREST

Homage to Lydia Cabrera

You want to kiss the moon? You want to know the truth?
It is no washing of deception in the ocean of this world.
The saints remake this so. The sand sucks up the water,
lets it go. And the coconut bares its shape, no matter
the answers of the night, the milk dripping from the stars.
The river is dark water, everyone knows that, it doesn't
reveal itself like a lagoon or that big tree you tried
to hide behind. The moon is not a girl, the river's
not a man. The fish wait for your lips when you're in muck.
They taste first, then they bite. The saints open
the road to great sinning. You have to be cared for
when stepping on the shadow bigger than the tree.
There are horses here and there's a field you never go in
where they grow pieces of you, shards and slivers
of what you're born to. The temper suits you.
 All the time a slow insect climbs up the wall,
spiky legs, feelers clicking, saying something to you,
going back to the day your aunt cut the water
snake in half with her machete,
back to the mosquito that sucked your blood,
back to your mama's big wet breasts. Is that it?
Your mind's a mess, can't tell the difference between
lie and truth, what you want and what you don't.
You've got to learn the biscuit and the cream of it, choke
juice coming out your mouth. And when you get to dream
you'll know the difference between mystery and sin.
All you think about is in your suitcase, bunch of smoke.
Row out to the middle of the ocean and talk to the waves,
the foamy part. When you speak their language you learn

lie doesn't matter, truth doesn't matter. Singing.
Rocking. Watching the moon go to her place,
way up behind the sun, behind the milk your mama gave.
You solitude, you company, you all that stays.

THE FOOD OF THE GODS

Homage to Juan O'Farrill

It begins with cornmeal and okra,
lentils and butterflies under the ceiba tree
and cockroach cracklings when the wife
isn't ready with the beans and rice and the husband
hungry as a panther after hard work in the fields.
Plantain for strength to cut the overgrowth,
the undergrowth, the inner growth. Fish the dirty food,
throw that to the dogs.

The gods eat air, the gods eat hope.
I know a god who eats the hearts of men, and another
who sucks dry the wombs of women then lies
with full belly to rest and laugh at humans
on their way to death. There once was a goddess
who ate earth and one who cut off the penises
of angels and ate them dipped in gold.
There was a goddess who ate lead. Her children
couldn't chew her milk. And another who went
upward to the stars and gnawed on night.

Green guava gives you the runs and tamarind makes you
pucker up all day and night, you cannot say a word.
There is good grass for sweet breath and crazy weed
that turns you inside out and makes you see the sun as stone.
At dusk over the countryside a tenderness appears
that the gods sprinkle on their turtle soup.

Boiled yuca to make you old. Meat on the bone to make you wise.
Earthworms to make you young. The worst food is moon.
You shut your mouth, you let it pass, the gods say
it burns the heart and boils the blood. Morning dew is for the children.
Adults are fools who eat the plants on which it grows. Do so
at your own risk and hope no one is looking. Water from the river.
Water from the sea. Urine of roosters for the liver and urine of stallions
for the sex. Get it strong and straight like a royal palm. That's our tree,
that and the ceiba and the framboyán. Visions come and visions go.
How else to know we're blessed or damned? Flesh of unborn goat,
milk of their mothers and the guinea hen's hackles
fried in lard. Good for the eyes, good for the throat.
Boiled bones of owls and sparrows. You make the tea
then let it sit awhile. Sweet hibiscus for elusive happiness
and thorn bush flowers to rid yourself of broken love.

When the day comes, the gods blame us for eating wrong.
They point their fingers and laugh.
They send mosquito gods and scorpion gods
and snake gods and gods of pestilence and war to punish us,
to make us know who owns the world.
Who is that Christ? Who is that man with the red beard
and his clothes on fire? The beginning is cornmeal
and okra. The end is cornmeal and okra, gummy and hot,
in the forest, in the open field, in the river that goes forever
deep into the dark country.

THE HIGHWAY OF BLAZING CARS

There is babbling in poetry
as there is science.
Many times the din deafens.
Sometimes a stream runs
inside the child inside of you,
who leaned toward the night
as the world grew tall.

Today the sand prevails,
those gray mountains
(turning blue in the distance),
the dry smell like an oven.
All you do not know
gathers here. Deaf women,
disheveled men, the south wind,
spiders the size of hands.
Green is an instant.

So—a shorn bush
bristling like a mother,
the shaved stone,
days without shadow,
light about to scour you,
then, suddenly,
the highway of blazing cars.

SPRING AND MALL

Homage to WCW

In the puddle reflection
freed from the stone,

a light made gray
in the accretion of lethargy,

commerce, parking lot,
curl of clover leaf and exit ramp.

A draft of codices
pushes up from the south,

seas and thighs and heavy eyelids
sovereign through cold wind,

a flower rises
in the mist of New Jersey

(rasp of radiators, clang
of steam), awakes!

BOURGEOIS BLOOD OVER BROOKLYN

Ten tons of metal
chortle to Manhattan
at five times the speed of an octopus.

Wake Camus and warn him
of the lonely men in shirt sleeves
leaning out of windows.

Where there are flowers you'll find
rapid-fire teeth, spoiled mums,
ten tons of metal on the Bridge.

Some old guy fishing—big deal—
with a bucket full of slimy bait
and a sad wife wiping her nose with her sleeve.

I counted trucks on the BQE
then strolled through Williamsburg
on the Sabbath, quiet as the day of death,

as if faith had married fate
the night before and caused a ruckus
no one yet has come to pacify,

net even God with his thirty-three-
and-a-half fingers and his twenty-
thousand-leagues-under-the-sea tongue.

There was a sea slug slogging
through, there was a bastion
of interstices, a woman ribbed,

a semi-automatic laughter. No one
came to the door. Only here
and there a car blew smoke,

a light went on in a third-floor window,
just a smirk and twilight noise,
the sunset bleeding over Brooklyn Heights.

EIGHT ABLUTIONS

1.   Your eyes drop into the depths
        where a child is hiding.

2.   Herons standing over those waters,
        waves rippling out and in.

3.   Your words like jellyfish,
        blue and tendriled.

4.   Your eyes like stones.

5.   Hinges for stillness.

6.   Child afraid of the moon,
        afraid of God stamping
        across the floor of heaven.

7.   God and his constellations.

8.   You and your nebulae.

THE CHANGE

began on a farm in Pennsylvania,
the mist coming off the river

over the lip of the land to the field
where it surrounded the barn and then

surrounded him. Still dawn, the oak's gnarled
branches barely visible above his head.

Out of the whitish soup a frittering hum
like a liquid machine, a large eye looking out,

a small eye looking in, sweet scent
of honeysuckle, fog needles on his lips

and arms. The old rooster crowed.
A creature moved through the tall grass.

It made the mist open to the light,
it made the seer become the seen.

Points of Balance

2005

MANDATE

Go forth and copulate,
said the deist to the beasts,

his eyes fixed
on an interstellar point

somewhere between the end of self
and the beginning of poetry.

MIRAGE

I move from one language
to another. I dive

from a pool of water
to a pool of dreams,

from the fire of words
to the shadow beyond them.

THE COMPLICITY OF THE FAMILIAR

Love is
the grammar of solitude.

I turn on the radio,
a neighbor knocks at the door,

I multiply the distance
between me and desire.

CITYSCAPE 1

Let the aroma of need
waft across the river to New Jersey:

all the snow and hills,
a sky that moves and moves.

I saw a rose in the clouds,
I saw happiness on fire.

FACT AND FAMINE

The streets are filled with non-cars,
non-buildings, non-people.

I think of your face
through the waste and the crowds

(hungry, impeded), the thousand
shards of sleep between us.

TOURNIQUETS AND ALL

The little self grew big,
the narrow curve relented.

You sliced into the butter of my longing.
Then. Now? The island

flashes like a knife, the dead
are swimming in my shadow.

CITYSCAPE 2

The glandular air
of November sweeps through

with little to offer
except the Hudson at five o'clock,

the black ships passing,
the lights of Verrazano on the map.

PURPOSE AND EXTRAVAGANCE

Wounded cross
and the statuary of broken angels,

I am open hearted.
Into me swing your wrecking

ball, your arraignments, yours
forever, plane encrusted.

CITYSCAPE 3

A red light over the city,
our solitudes ringing.

Here I am (an interval),
there you are (an equinox).

We go where the wind grows.
We enter the hollows of autumn.

DRESS REHEARSAL

This city is a French
horn in distress.

Calvin chasing hens
and the pages of the hymnal blank

like a furious whoosh,
a stomach pain, the pitch of sin.

CITYSCAPE 4

The heart fast beating,
tenure of grief, of unknowing.

Bird swoops out of the cliffs
to the old factory.

Stranded on the next page
the arthropod sun is rising.

EX LIBRIS

Childhood was Cervantes,
adulthood flared with Hemingway.

I look for death in every book,
intertextual, salivary:

what the ocean says
and says again and then forgets.

ARS POETICA

What do you know
about poetry?

What do you know
about the last grain

of the last meal of rice
on the universe of your plate?

RUSSIAN DOLL

Every wall is an eye,
every eye is a wall.

I have only myself tonight
in a language inside a language

about the white sky falling
and the black earth.

BREVIARY

And when I run out of things
to say, what do I say?

And when the thrush sings
in the know-it-all woods,

isn't there a slippage
from language to departure?

AMOR VINCIT OMNIA

So this is where the cunning
coney lives.

Look at it come close, go far,
cross highways, reach the sea,

its ambidextrous eyes
leaping (perpendicular) like fish.

TECTONICS OF THE IMPERCEPTIBLE

I sit at my desk
waiting for you.

My heart (quick hound)
jumps to a memory:

blue land (your face),
around it the ocean of sleep.

HAVANA DREAM

The red eye blinks and it is you
(in between the rain),

out of the crumbling rooms,
a note played on the piano,

a salt wind off the ocean,
lonely, refracted (you).

I CARRY YOU WITH ME

to the silence store, the scream shop,
the bureau of solitude. My pockets

are lined with you-bills, my nostrils
with you-smells. You knocked at my door

and I sent you away. Look at me now
swimming in you-ness.

TECHNIQUE OF WHAT

What is the snow
and flotsam on the bed?

What is the flatness of waking?
What are the dry throats of starlings

(quick, cowardly)
calling for, greenery or death?

BEFORE THE SOLUTIONS

In the boxes a year's supply
of moods (bovine, sublunary).

I hear them out,
I hear them in.

Now tone on the street,
new tone, same boxes.

VENUS IN VARADERO

The sea is chaste with many minds.
One is naked (she walks

out of the waves). Another
invented silence (her hair becomes

the wind). The third remembers
the music (before it was a song).

SMOKE AND MIRRORS IN HAVANA

The sea in its immensity
is telling a story.

Here is darkness (long
long train through the night).

There under the carpet, grandmother
dust, grandfather consequence.

END OF THE AFFAIR

Funny how the fun collapses,
archaic, blended into threnody.

Funny how we dream of hoping
and go back to the books,

the dusty shelves. (Funny how)
our patience lapses.

The Floating Island

1999

THE FLOATING ISLAND

*. . .brillando contra el sol y contra los poetas. . . ***

—Heberto Padilla

There it is, the long prow
of the Caribbean, charging to break
the map's complexion.
It is a key, a crocodile, a hook,
an uncoiling question,
a stretch of sinews catching
dribbles from the continent
under which it will forever float.

The island mouth is smiling
or frowning, who can tell,
stuffed with waning intentions,
sugarcane and sand.

Such a little place, such
an island listing against sorrow
in the middle of the ocean's gut,
playing make believe
queen of brine, dressing up in green
and calling forth its poets for praise,
its leaders for chesty boasts,
inventing for itself a pantheon
of tropical saints, a vast
and profound literature,
an epic history to rival Rome's.

There it is, pretending it shimmers
over the heads of its people,
denying the terror it feels
when no one listens, denying
that it is always almost drowning,
that it cannot help anyone,
least of all itself, that it is only
a strip of dirt between morning and night,
between what will be and what was,
between the birth of hope
and the death of desire.

* *Shining against the sun and against poets.*

THE LOVE OF BLONDES

I don't know what I would be
if there were no Cuba,
if there were no childhood,
no Malecón or José Martí,
no sharks in the water or hot car
seat sticking to the underthighs
midafternoon, no Jaimanitas where we fished,
La Playa where we swam,
no Constellation gunning its engines
over the Tropic of Cancer,
if we hadn't left behind a frown,
a sweet and sour pill,
the arroz con frijoles of politics and laughter.

What if I woke one morning
and I was Serbian or Senegalese
or star-spangled American?
When I think everything is in control
I remember the day my father
took me to a ball game in el Cerro
—Habana against Almendares—
and he put five on the home team
and bought me a peanut cone
and I saw the Cuban flag waving
in front of all that blue sky.
I was the happiest boy on earth,
I thought I had entered eternity,
I thought el Cerro was Paradise
and the ball players were angels

and God was Bicicleta, the obese
ball retriever, JJ the bet taker
a manic John the Baptist. And then as JJ ran
to the numbers man waving money
and stumbling, the blonde appeared,
sliding down the steps to the box seats,
tall and tanned and movie liquid,
making the vendors stop their hawking
and the men in the stands
hold their arguments and fat Bicicleta
turn away from foul balls.
Over the stadium came a silence
it had never known, every man there joined
in admiration, adulation
and longing for the blonde in blue
just then sitting down, letting the sun
illuminate the freckles on her shoulder.
And I, we, became blasphemers, idolaters,
Bicicleta paling beside this sun goddess,
this saint of salivation, this Helen of elation.
From that point on Paradise
was no longer el Cerro but the steps
she trod, the dress she wore,
the chair she sat on, the country
of her birth, the polis of her pubis.

I ate of the fruit of baseball and beauty.
The land faded, happiness disappeared
and I realized my loss—
el Cerro forgotten, JJ in a wheelchair,
Bicicleta dead and I don't know
what would happen if there were no Cuba
and I was someone else,
living in Dakar or Indianapolis
next door to the blonde,
she always calling me over for coffee
and I obliging.

THE LABYRINTH OF HEARING

Is the function of the poet here mere sound...?
—Wallace Stevens, "Academic Discourse at Havana"

Sound no,
but the root of sound.
Delight, or else the certainty of words
linking in the patter of thought,
eloquence to bring the sea
back into the heart, the spirit's
tenor into landscape.

There was a sky, blue,
and an earth, red and green,
to make all other colors bow to sound
and the poet cull them as he went
for dream or nightmare, pestilence
or plenitude, sea breeze or cyclone.

There never was water
in the poet's mirth
or compassion for the destitute.
Rather mockingbird and lizard,
rather fish and undulance
and ebb of intellect.

There never was a sea
lapping at bare feet
or damp downed thighs
on which his lips might dance.

There never was a function here.
The poet spoke for no one's sake,
no one died, no one was saved,
but eyebrows flickered out of boredom,
bellies rippled under linen,
an echo quivered through
the labyrinth of hearing.

CALLE AMARGURA

In Havana there is a street called Calle Amargura or Bitterness Street

On Bitterness Street
a man runs from the rain
arms raised into the next imagination.

A woman sits head down
on the stoop of a house
where her indiscretions
fly about like butterflies.

All songs end,
memories soar over rooftops,
an eyelid swells with desire.

On Bitterness Street,
Calle Amargura, there are boys
holding their tongues,
they dare not speak, they await
their turn in the line of understanding.

On that street
a daughter is dying.
Her father searches for a cure
and finds instead the pillar of his wife,
covered with lizard scales,
melting with the rain.

On Bitterness Street,
Calle Amargura, no one is surprised
at the awful taste of Paradise.

THE FOREIGNER'S SONG

This is how I dress my face
to mask the waterfall of fear.

This is how I tame my lips to lie
flat on the bone, obedient before you.

My voice no longer trembles.
It chirps like a sparrow or a door hinge.

This is how I learn your crevices,
the noise-like silence of your bells,

your words for sex, whim,
eyes cold as blue stains.

Look at my neck and shoulders, so gallant.
I have trained them too like a saint

to lift and turn from strangers,
my countrymen, to wait and wait.

Who will know I have cut myself off
from the breeze, the odors of youth?

Who will care that my song
(the song you gave me)

leaves no trace and drifts off to sea
where only a mockingbird listens?

I have grown new feet, they are dainty.
I have kissed a new tongue,

it is marble. I no longer speak of loss.
I know nothing of Paradise (the pants I wear

are too long), I am constantly eating
my vowels, my throat is sore.

A child sits on the curb waiting for me.
Soon he will turn away.

CARTOGRAPHY

The map speaks.
Speaks of time and warped waists.
Continents sing numbers
of the underneath and sand.
Sand whispers in the belly is
the snake. The snake appears on the next
land mass. The mass has no waist
but flutters when I breathe. The sea
is flat and of one depth
like the land. The land is wide where I sit
and stamp my feet. The snake uncoils
and spits at the sky.
The sky is not on the map.

PHILADELPHIA

The coffee has redeemed itself by now.
I am awake enough to see you walking
down the street to your apartment
exhausted like a sparrow
after long work in the tenements.

You linger in my memory hunched a little,
tragic, hurt by men. The afternoon haze
is café con leche in the city,
the block busy with unemployed
latinos, sipping beer, playing
dominoes, whispering deals at the corner.

Across the street the huge Lithuanian
church has become ridiculous.
Hardly anyone enters. Rhythm and form
fly away with the pigeons
and the river is a slab of dirty wood.
You turn the corner, disappear.
Philadelphia is awash in loss.
This is the dream the coffee drowned.

NOCTURNO DE WASHINGTON

*As the XVth century Chinese scholar Xiangyen Zhixian swept the path
to his shack, a pebble hit a stalk of bamboo and at that moment he
achieved the enlightenment he had searched for all his life.*

1.

They called forth the train whistle at midnight,
the end of October, the wrecking ball month.
They called forth the snow and it came in ricochets,
singes of ancient fires.

They suited up. They brought home
bacon and oranges, the twelve-month year,
the lawns of the wealthy, the shacks of the poor.
God gave his blessing and it was good.

They made the twelve tribes and the rabbit ears,
the cemeteries, tractor trailers, parakeets,
the ivory trade, the undersea stones, pews
and pencils, commuter lines at dawn.

They stopped, looked out over the vast creation,
saw the empty fields covered with weeds,
the gutters glutted with bottles, the board
rooms with barrel-chested har, har, har.

They recycled empties, restored the ruins
of Hollywood props, they colorized Ava Gardner's
lips, Bogart's ashen skin, pulled levers,
made bridges rise and mountains disappear.

A sailing ship sailed on, corazón, corazón,
down to the bottom of the ocean, the darkest amplitude,
the starkest drowning. The captain wrote
"Rocks and sharks have come upon us unaware."

They called forth flamingoes and the third race
at Hialeah when the two-year-old filly stumbled
and broke a leg. They called forth compassion,
a bullet through the brain,

loved the right things right
then went home before intolerance,
"so without all manhood, emptie of all pity..."
and the dirty fingernails of wisdom.

They called forth hunger, the Western wind,
a peg-legged woman sleeping on a park bench
(Walker Evans, Havana, 1933). They called forth
dust bowls and bread lines, tenements and ideology.

They brought up children and long rains,
longer droughts, 17,000 wars to end all wars, old men
cooked in greed, the buzzard hubris pecking out
the eyes of saints, América la grande, América en pavor.

They called forth the left and called forth
the right, wrote down the seven moralities,
the twenty amenities, signed manifestoes,
sold condoms on credit, pantyhose to patriarchs.

They joined a long line of indigents
wanting tickets to Paradise, but the show
was sold out. They invoked bilge and arbitrage,
an ignorance like prairie fire,

whimpers intertwining,
una niña azul bañada en la tristeza, Bleed
America, Inc., breach in the stone, Bleed America,
Inc., hymen broken, leaf abstracted,

and the river glass-like, silent,
slithering through travesty, and the rats
in the tenements chewing and contemplating,
blinking and defecating.

2.

At midnight the Washington Monument rises.
Here in the clouds is the cusp
of power it says to the snow whirling down,
here is the center of all matter.

Let no one mistake our intent, let no one
come here doubting the limits of our strength:
perpetuity, policy like glass, unblemished,
invariable. The monument stands beyond, before all.

The president is asleep, his cabinet is asleep,
the people's representatives, every one under covers.
Only a scholar up late with his books fixes coffee,
looks out the window, wonders when the snow will end.

In the distance the train whistle bleats.
The sky is falling on government, wasting itself
on mall and monument. The scholar thinks
knowledge is nothing, knowing is all.

Night everywhere, leaving its dust under fingernails,
behind ears. Night filling up with snow,
replicating sleep. Night of tantrum
songs and howling dogs and tears.

Night the substance of solitude,
the bucket of fog, the insomnia overcoat.
Night the misanthrope, the ambidextrous,
lipless laughter, empty room.

If there is no option, let the winter come.
If there is no residue, let the haunches grow.
If the past does not billow to the future, let the ship
be shoaled and the cold muffle the nightmare hum.

The scholar sits in yellow light.
He thinks of wife and children, the parents
he left behind, the jasmine in the garden,
the river flowing past his fishing line,

the places of his dreams, the offices and roads,
the city and the sea: one life, one moment
out of which grows the need, the calling,
the sound of a pebble swept against a bamboo stalk.

ASBURY PARK

Between heaven and hell there is nothing but us.
——A bar patron, Asbury Park, New Jersey

Between the jetty and the haze
is the churn of the waves,
a broken down merry-go-round,

a grinning clown on the funhouse wall.
Between the convention hall and the long brick pier
is an orange and blue minigolf

and plastic palm trees stripped of fronds,
a breeze picking up
and the cold bone of winter returning.

Between human failure and God's defeat
is the faint scent of the ozone of catastrophe,
something fallen out of the sky,

torn Astroturf, a peeling Howard Johnson,
two patrons inside drinking beer.
Here the water of the ocean,

there the ocean of the mind,
here the seagull on the beach,
there the one in our dreams, circling

a nostalgia for what never was.
Between the Gulf Stream and the North Atlantic,
empire and gold leaf, wallet and silage, is

the damp morning sunshine, one false step
to heaven, the certain step into hell.
Between the blackbird and the telephone wire,

strollers on the high-banked beach
and long black ships passing by,
coming and going are the same.

In this space everything fits:
pigeons fornicating on the boardwalk,
two old men on bikes wearing umbrella hats,

looking papal and somber and analogous,
and all around is the sea,
roiling, frothing, massive, smelling

like an army of horseshoe crabs,
a soup of eyes and algae.
Between the moon rose rising

and the blood of dawn before it spills,
between a shadow on the forehead
and the grass stalks in gold fire,

between the jewels of night
and the children laughing in the flames,
we breathe, we drown, we scuttle on.

THE MOUNTAIN

The day is a remark made of clouds,
a walk up the mountain past a leaning trailer,
a path through the darkening woods.

The day is a mockingbird
swooping to a fence post, the wind
upside down shaking the hilltops.

The day is leaf fritter
and blossoming laurel,
the day flings itself into the rain.

The day hobbles, the rain thinks:
a man is alone on the path,
his mother dead a month.

In the valley the river meanders,
the day sits on the bank under a willow,
tugs its ear, remembers an empty house,

a woman coughing over her soup,
her comb dropped on the hospital floor
as she was wheeled away.

There is no end to the grief that is given,
the joy that is taken, whatever life
remains in the black spring earth.

The day plunges down a ravine,
climbs out the other side
to the place beyond ruins,

imagines a car parked at the end of the road,
lovers making American love, her toes
stretching for pleasure, his lips at her breast,

her hand at the root where he thrives,
where he grows, where he dies. The day
is a mammal running away

through the ferns, a stone
the man picks up, throws at a shadow
in the bush, a bare branch teetering.

The day is no longer day
but a trash heap, a dog coiled and sleeping,
a clothes' washer rusting.

The day is oak in profusion and maple
and spruce and wild lettuce by a rotting log,
the terms and lineaments of solitude,

the shape of night, confronting a mystery:
how the path leads away from the self,
how the self leads away from the light.

The day is a man in the forest
under the rain, unpacified by sleep
or mother's breast or lunge of sex.

He is passing through, waiting
for the trees to fall away, the path to open
on a field that stretches to the sea.

A POEM FOR THE EPIPHANY

It snows because the door to heaven is open,
because God is tired of working
and the day needs to be left alone.
It snows because there is a widow hiding
under her mother's bed,
because the birds are resting their throats
and three wise men are offering gifts.
Because the clouds are singing
and trees have a right to exist,
because the horses of the past are returning.
They are gray and trot gently into the barn
never touching the ground.

It snows because the wind wants
to be water, because water
wants to be powder and powder
wants to seduce the eye. Because once
in his life the philosopher has to admit
to the poverty of thought.
Because the rich man cannot buy snow
and the poor man has to wear it on his eyebrows.

Because it makes the old dog think
his life has just begun. He runs
back and forth across the parking lot.
He rolls on the snow. He laps it up.

It snows because light and dark
are making love in a field where old age
has no meaning, where colors blur,
silence covers sound, sleep covers sorrow,
everything is death, everything is joy.

Arching into the Afterlife

1991

THE GATES OF HELL

after Rodin

1.

No one knows what is beyond them
or when they will open
or if he's already in.

A father gnaws at his sons,
lovers lunge outward
to escape, and the rest boil
in the knowledge of their damning.

2.

The damned give shadows so smooth,
so rounded, he who shaped them
must have known sinew,
curve and plane as he knew sin.

Every form is light
dulled into despair.
Love or its disguise leads here:
failed grasping.

Here we recognize
the moment darkness made us
bend and touch our heels,
know loss, our father's breath,
the bite of consciousness.

3.

The Thinker sits over us,
central, hunched,
not at peace with thought
but not in agony.

His shoulders hold a concentration,
a leveling, balance without delight,

almost a hope
that somewhere night is ebbing.

FULTON FISH MARKET

The curve of the island
and the smell have brought me here,
the day's catch just in from the sea

and I happen on this gathering of eyes,
heads, tails to see spines tangle
in stiff battles, pale fillets lick
boxfuls of crushed ice.

Send for the fishmonger,
ask for the meaning of fish
when they die—
bubbles of blood on the gills
like romantic poets.

In the bottom of the box
there is usually a fluttering.
I would like to believe
under all that cold
a heart fights for water.

The fishmonger loves
my whooshing from world to world,
pouting at the sun,
shivering with silence.

Blind hunger is the best bait

he declares from his chair—
ruler of bones and salt,
flesh-lord of the universe.

The box is still.
The Brooklyn Bridge arches into the afterlife.

VIEW DOWNRIVER

Trenton Makes. The World Takes.

That bridge is a poem,
he said donning his jacket
as the wind whipped up the leaves.

Trenton makes.

The world
doesn't know beauty.
The river shows its teeth
ready to swallow children.

Takes
a blind eye,
a man
ready to drop at the factory door.
Balls it's cold, he said.

Takes knowing
what those letters say,

a few beers
not to see the bed at night,
the wife spread open
like a crusty beach,
daughters polishing their nails,
laughing at his pitted teeth.

Takes giving up,
a chance to die in peace.
No questions asked.

THE IVORY TOWER

It has taken a long time
and the tusks of many elephants.
It is not a conspicuous place—
straight and simple
by a calm clean river.
It is surrounded by moderate woods.
On the horizon a cloud or two
roll gently by.
Birds, of course:
hawks, thrushes, doves.
The cliffs behind it
add mystery and the degree of solitude
by which one measures God.
Beyond the cliffs there is lightning
and barbarous armies clashing.
There is also poverty and despair
and frowns scuttling across deserts
and all manner of sins growing
gnarled and knotted from the earth.
Do not dwell on this.
The daffodils are coming up
by the marble bench. Let us go
and pick them.

CROSSING

A field of snow.
You can only look across it for so long.
You could go blind.
You could freeze. You could
turn back and leave it
cold and brilliant as the hand of God.
At the end you imagine a lover,
a parent, someone
who ignored you years ago.
So you throw yourself
into the field and walk, slowly at first,
feline, stalking.

Soon the anxiety becomes unbearable
like cold or brilliance. You run,
you scream, you fall, your mouth
fills with snow, you get up,
you try to weep, the field
is wider than you thought—
go on, crawl if you must.

Now you're close. A few yards away
you say, Surprise!
The face turns and it has your eyes,
your nose, your mouth panting,
cold, almost blind. Behind you,
at the edge of the unspoiled field,
a dim figure stamps its feet—
parent, lover, someone,
acres of snow between you.

SAM'S DELI, SOUTH BROAD

The tall man with the hair
cut straight across the forehead
lounges smoking cigarettes.

You don't even get a napkin
with your hamburger.

I remember a girl long ago
I made love to with my socks on.

Some twist of life
brought Sam, bristled and grubby,
to this landmark of grease
in the gut of Trenton.

The tall man asks for a Klondike
bar, then the usual for lunch.

I remember the bitter cold outside
and her gasps like a bellows on the couch.

A cat drifts among Styrofoam towers.
Love was surrender then, and now

South Broad, no napkin, ketchup
dripping out of the bun.

IRON DUST

This close to spring
there is no more news
worth waiting for under
the light of the 7/11 parking lot.

No truth beyond
the dirty blond boy
slapping the video game
by the charcoal bags
or the tee-shirted enormity
of the cashier's breasts,
milk in the cooler,
Playboy, Hot Rod, Hustler,
Easy Rider, Sporting News.

And the fog is white
not yellow, and it's
more like breath not
a cat, more like stomach,
the soul of someone
who went to hell on a dare
and touched the underknee of God.

North is Calvintown.
South is Trenton,

Route 31,
all the stations
closed or closing, the car
out of gas running on hope
and the convenient coffee
like iron-dust soup.

STATE COMPLEX

Steeples rise with chimneys and bureaucracies
to dim the sun. The river is forgotten, horizontal.
The city lavishes upon itself the clarity of numbers.
The temples resemble offices, the offices
resemble prisons, the prisons resemble factories.
After all these years and marble steps
only the river knows where it goes,
or cares not, following the pull of gravity.

In the park I think of ancient Chinese poets
so distant from the stains of history.
They knew their fallacies and drank their wine
while winds wore pavilions down to stone
and scattered the imperial dreams of permanence
they celebrated.

Wisp of smoke. Ripple of rapids and curve of light
over the bank. At dusk the weeds and garbage
gain distinction. The structures hum in Sunday rest,
yellow like urine or gold. God a huge cat
slinks through parking lots and autumn
strokes the avenues. The night pours out like water.

JERSEY NIGHTS

CAMDEN

Something secret raced down the street
and left a smell behind—
a rose in heaven, a cat long dead.

Someone hung intestines from electric lines,
nuzzled a gravestone,
tasted the ashes of apple pies.

I saw boys straddled on fences
looking for manhood
and women with eyes for pigeons.
Their brains were full of knives,
their hearts were full of feathers.

In Camden just under the wind
I heard the sighs of an old poet waking.
He sensed the meaning of chimneys,
he sang until the factories whimpered
and the willows turned up their branches
and the ruins turned to butterflies.

Out of the marsh,
out of the center of the function
of things, out of the arcing roadway
and the roaring trucks, out of the drainpipe
as the snow melts and purifies the dark,
out of the itchy poets and the pest
control deputies and the organized men
lounging in their dream canoes and ladies
in fur coats dripping with mustard,
out of the blue light of blindness, the city rises

gorged on best intentions, sucking
the teat of the mother of dawn,
Newark of a little laughter, a little
light, a little beer on the stoop,
a little jazz in the stairwell,

Newark hoping for some rain, some flood
left over, grateful of the work
that fills the spaces between love,
facing the spot where the sun rises,
the sea makes waves, a girl
sucking on a lollipop is looking down the boulevard.

TRENTON

Deep winter night.
The tongues of the Common quivered—
the salt tongues
and the bitter tongues,
the tongues of the dreams of Hungarians,
the tongues of widows sealing envelopes
for their husbands,
tongues of macadam,
pine barren tongues,
tongues of poets and politicians
battling one another with mirrors.

I met a woman
cradling a stone in her arms.
The doctor found it by her bladder
waiting for light.
She walked on singing.
Her talisman cracked.

When the snows come
they stay for days,
when the snows leave
the night wounds heal.

The highways point
to states of concrete,
waves, golden corn.

Love, the nest under rushes
by the ice-jammed river.

TO THE MUSE

Here on your nape is the thinnest vein
where meaning gathers. Here on your shoulders
is the sweat of summer. I taste it like wine,
like sleep. There is no mend to winter's tear,
there is no end to this tomorrow.

I am tired of watching the moon spill on my hands,
I am tired of my bones in the morning,
the monotone of work and wires.

Once there were no sounds and the earth
rested round and satisfied. The river
spoke the language of wells and loam or none at all.

I grow deaf on purpose. The moon is mother
to my age. There could be love but it
would be a word. There could be hope
and it would be a mouth or milk or briers.

The answer is a stone, a city of locked doors,
the storm in your breast turned fog and in the fog
dead coal and in the night a mouthful of ashes.

Every road leads out. Birds gather
dust and fish swim up the stair.
I'll go. The greener side of dreams
is in the world. Your vein leads there.

NOCTURNE

There is wind in the trees,
black sound of owls under stars:
I return to the motions of the seas.

The moon slips through the waves,
la antigua relación entre palabra y musgo.
The wind rails at the trees,

what first gave light to incense
and myrtle at the entrance to shadows—
I return there always

to the brunt of bone that spawns
the arteries of summer, spider to its bed,
the wind to its image in the trees.

Thin-legged so the evening is,
green leaves flailed by weather
and the motions of the seas.

Dangerous and loving, old as death,
antigua araña: palabra, musgo, sleep and fire.
Wind in the trees!
I return to the motions of the seas.

THE DAUGHTER OF MEMORY

Long time ago
                    on the beach
the girl in the sequined
                    swimsuit
called me behind a pillar
                    for a dime I could
see her pull the crotch
                    of the suit
to one side watch the puffy
                    hairless seam
fold on itself. I paid the price.
                    I keep on
paying it—something about
                    the communion
of silver and flesh
                    in the shadows
that's kept me here
                    all these years.

Pork Rind and Cuban Songs

1975

EL CABALLERO DE PARIS

*El Caballero de Paris—Le Monsieur de Paris—roamed for many years
the streets of the city. The resort of angry mothers whose children refused to
eat their dinners, his fame spread like the summer sun through the
imaginations of all of us.*

Out of goodness,
out of belief in that legend,
the man let his scalp and face
produce a strain of hair
whiter than the blooms of roses
growing out of his arms,

he wore his toga made
of dirty bedsheets
the good priests bestowed on him

and set to walking streets
citing Bible passages
to any passerby who dared to listen
and those who mocked
the madness he regaled in.

Ever since the Sunday walk
on the Malecón that busy day
when my mother pointed to his face
and beard becoming one
with the wind, I grew terrified
of prophets and white hair.

Whenever he passed our yard
I would hide behind the heat of bushes
and watch him peel the one orange
he'd ever accept from grandmother's
hand then wait until his sheets
made him a butterfly next to the sea.

Now, after his commitment
to a State Hospital that erased him
from the witchwaters of Havana streets
and eventually to death,
of which no one, not even the priests,
was sorry, I have grown used to him:
to his habits, to his proffered rose,
to the sandals that gathered up
the soil I longed to grow on.

THE TAÍNO'S ELEGY TO HIMSELF

The sun is setting as it has
every day of my life.
No one can change it now,
bring it back or ask it never
come again.

The Caribs have come, hungry
and wise. They are warriors.
They will not take all of us,
only enough for the feast;
the rest will be assured
their lives for yet another year.

My wife is with the other women.
The fiercest will taste
her tenderness and her milk
(the womb is a delicacy
they cook in lizard oil).

My children are reserved
for the chief, who will pick
their bones like those of a fleshy
chicken wing.

The sun sets over us,
over my Taíno blood that told me
not to kill at the expense
of my own flesh, that taught me
peace at the expense of my own
freedom.

The sun sets as it always has
and I can now safely believe in darkness.

SATURN DEVOURING HIS CHILDREN

after Goya

The god sat hungry,
showing teeth like muscles.
The sweat of his gums
ran
dribbling
down
      his chest.
His latest son produced
prepared
      in a rare sweet
blood sauce
      lay
raw and bland
      for him.
He bit into the child
      head first
to swallow as much
      tender boy as
his one opprobrious bite
      allowed him
choking with blond fat
      pleasurably.

Saturn chanced a look ahead
and terrified he saw
the artist
recording
what he someday would hang
on his dining wall
over the heads of his guests.

THE FRUGAL REPAST

after Picasso

The man looks away
into the blueness of his shadow
daring it to approach
the woman he holds.

Her breasts are sagging but attractive,
her eyes look into themselves:
she has swallowed her darkness
and turned its color.

A hand is pasted on her shoulder—
she wonders
if it is really his,
she dreams
of a better meal with a better man.

Maybe it is his shadow
she'd give into.

WEST FOURTH STREET SUBWAY STATION: 4AM

1.

It is not that I'm afraid.
I'm just bored
of sitting
without people or fear,
watching the vending machine
wait for fingers and coins.

2.

Hugo, el Puertorrican,
once told me he loved subways.
He would sit in the station
and take no train.
The man selling tokens got nervous,
so he was asked to leave.

Two days before I saw him last.

3.

I have a companion:
A lady walks to the phone booth,
draws the doors
and sits. No call.
It is better there?

Shhh.
Sound is coming.
The quake cracking open
the mouth of the tunnel!

Forget it, Hugo.
I'm going home.

NINE FOR MINA

1.

She's the first one up
inching seventy-five years of weight
down younger stairs
to make a morning's ration
of café cubano,
the almost black, almost syrup
breakfast she's made an only habit of.

"Buenos días"
coffee dripping down the sides
of the offered cup.

2.

"We had sixteen hundred acres,
half sugarcane, half grazing land,
half papaya and avocados
and the rest wild.

"Your grandfather would ride out
like a king on his bay horse,
the one you saw on the pasture
before leaving,
and I would wave him off.
At five in the morning
he was a strong and a beautiful man."

3.

The three of us watched
from the porch after dinner
an overloaded cane wagon
pull its oxen up on hind legs
by the rings on their nostrils.
There was genuine anguish
there that day.

Grandfather called across the way.
He screamed.
The men didn't know what to do.
He rushed to the road
and pulled a handful of cane off the cart,
and another, and then another,
until the beasts touched ground.
Some still had cud in their mouths.

4.

A twitch around the horse's upper lip.
The eyes of terror,
the ropes around the hind legs
that dropped him.

Grandfather, with the clean knife
and the yellow smelling cure,
rolled its testicles gently in his hands,
sensing their ripeness perhaps.
I felt a buzzing in my own.

Quickly he peeled the skin
as he would from his midday fruit.
The horse trembled
and the red gorgeous seeds saw the sun.

There was one last look at them.
Then he sliced and ran.
The black hell of hide exploded.
Pulled men to the ground.
Wailed in horse, stood and stumbled.
His chin hit the dirt,
the eyes bulged with the death inside.
He fell with his pride
and let out a pant of exhaustion.

5.

Nearing noon
the men stopped cutting.
The cane would rest in the heat;
they went home to lunch and shade.
It was the quiet of field and breeze,
it was the rustle of prickly leaves,
it was the yellow and green
of the huge heaps of cane I watched
before the slash and whip of machetes
and the black sweat
of muscled labor and the raspy voice
of the foreman on his horse
drove me away.

6.

Mina plucked chickens for supper;
the quick flick of the wrist
made down in the kitchen
after the lightning wrench
of the neck and the soak
in scalding water like the heat outside,
feather-mad looks came out of her sallow face.

7.

While frying pork rind
she heard of grandfather's fall
from his horse as he came home alone.
He lay there for hours
until a girl sent for fruit
found the body and brought him.

8.

In Havana,
in the cool of the lucid and great hospital
where doctors performed miracles
for sick farmers
he had cancer.
The doctors went in,
cut away, and closed him up.
He was healthy again
(three thousand pesos' worth of health),
the tumor and the prostate
in the garbage can.

They gave him six months.
He took six years
until he fell again, this time in bed,
and was watched as he panted
and raved
and died.

9.

Now in North Jersey,
having lost all those acres
and her husband,
with nerves like mud puddles,
her mind barely floating
on the sparse milk of her hair,
she too dies.
Slowly, painlessly,
bringing coffee to us
when we need it.

THE PASSAGE FROM THE VIRGIN TO THE BRIDE

after Marcel Duchamp

is brown with some green
arms flexed toward
a creaking bed in a cheap hotel.

What are lines when lost in color?
Transition.
There is no white in this work,
only a pasty undoing
dripping into untrodden cubicles.

A leg slips,
falls out of place
and the hues strain
not to say
anything has changed.

THE DREAM OF ICARUS

Artfully (they say)
wax and muscle
shining
grazing a lonely cloud
a feather now
I fly away
from the minotaur's land
and reach for
the hand of my father
coming
out of the sun.

CARTAGENA DE INDIAS

The woman balancing
a tree-load of fruit on her head
sings the song of pulp
that wakes me.

The fan blades overhead
as if the heat were something
to be cut down.

The pillow sticks to my face.
You'd figure I was eating
mangoes all night long.

POVERTY DOESN'T STOP ON WEEKENDS

A boy comes every day by my window
when the garbage is out and sinks
into it, diving for usables, snouting
for food pigs think twice before eating.
He is of one mind,
the stomach, that dreams for him
alley cat dreams. Today there were
carnations that wouldn't glow
anymore. Five years into the business
of living, he smelled them
and picking the fairest, went
on down the street of an early
Saturday morning.

Acknowledgments

Over the years I have been graced with the friendship and support of many people, too many to list here. Fred Arroyo, Gregory Orfalea, and Mark Statman read versions of this collection and offered sound advice and suggestions. To them a special thank you.

I also offer my gratitude to Steven Huff and Philip Memmer of Tiger Bark Press for their careful work in preparing the manuscript for publication.

My son Pablo A. and my sister Silvia and her four sons have accompanied me along the way.

My partner Kassie Rubico protects, borders, and greets me daily. I am a lucky man.

The following magazines, newspapers, and anthologies were generous enough to publish some of the poems collected in this book:

The Americas Review, American Poetry Review, Analog Sea, Artful Dodge, Barrow Street, Black Swan Review, The Cincinnati Review, Connotation Press, Contact II, The Emerson Review, Five AM, Five Points, Florida Review, Hanging Loose, Harvard Review on-line, The Hollins Critic, Kansas Quarterly, Linden Lane Magazine, Leon, Locomotive, Miami Monthly, Minimus, New Letters, Nightsun, Notre Dame Review, Palmetto Review, The Paterson Literary Review, Pivot, The Plum Review, poem-a-day, Poet Lore, Poetry, Post Road, Provincetown Arts, Querkus, Redivider, The Reston Review, The Same, Seneca Review, Subtropics, The Sycamore Review, Tar River Poetry, and *Terra Poetica.*

Bluestones and Salt Hay; Cuban American Writers: Los Atrevidos; The Body Electric: The Best Poetry from The American Poetry Review; Burnt Sugar; The Ecco

Anthology of International Poetry; Joy: 100 Poems; Hammer and Blaze; Little Havana Blues; The Norton Anthology of Latino Literature; 110 Stories: New York Writes about 9/11; Outsiders; Paper Dance; poem-a-day 365 Poems for Every Occasion; Shade 2004; US 1: An Anthology; WPFW Poetry Anthology.

And I am unspeakably grateful to the publishers of the following books, where these poems appeared:

Pork Rind and Cuban Songs. NuClassics and Science Publishing Co. 1975.
Arching into the Afterlife. Bilingual Review Press. 1991.
The Floating Island. White Pine Press. 1999.
Points of Balance / Puntos de apoyo. Four Way Books. 2005.
The Man Who Wrote on Water. Hanging Loose Press. 2011.
Calle Habana. Photostroud. 2013.
The Island Kingdom. Hanging Loose Press. 2015.
The Cuban Comedy. Unnamed Press. 2019.

About the Author

Cuban-born Pablo Medina is the author of nineteen books, most recently the novel *The Cuban Comedy* and the poetry collection *Soledades* (poems in Spanish). His critically acclaimed translations include García Lorca's *Poet in New York* (with Mark Statman) and Alejo Carpentier's seminal novel *The Kingdom of This World*. Medina's work has appeared in various languages and in magazines and periodicals throughout the world. Winner of many awards for his work, including fellowships from the Rockefeller Foundation, the National Endowment for the Arts, and the Guggenheim Foundation, Medina lives in Williamsville, Vermont, and is on faculty at the Warren Wilson MFA Program for Writers.

Colophon

The text of *The Foreigner's Song* is set in Perpetua.
This trade edition was printed by BookMobile in Minneapolis, MN.

Publication of this book was made possible through the generous
contributions of the following donors:

The Bishop Butler Society

Laure-Anne Brown

Charles Cote

Stephen Kuusisto

Tony Leuzzi

Georgia Popoff

John Skoyles

David Weiss

Nancy White

MORE POETRY FROM TIGER BARK PRESS

Old Horse, What Is to Be Done? by Stephen Kuusisto
The Half-Life, by Roger Greenwald
Psychometry, by Georgia A. Popoff
I Play His Red Guitar, by Charles Coté
Per Diem, by David Weiss
Boy on a Doorstep, by Richard Foerster
Totem: America, by Debra Kang Dean
After Morning Rain, by Sam Hamill
Meditation Archipelago, by Tony Leuzzi
Fancy's Orphan, by George Drew
Translucent When Fired, by Deena Linett
Ask Again Later, by Nancy White
Pricking, by Jessica Cuello
Dinner with Emerson, by Wendy Mnookin
As Long As We Are Not Alone, by Israel Emiot,
translated by Leah Zazulyer
Be Quiet, by Kuno Raeber, translated by Stuart Friebert
Psalter, by Georgia A. Popoff
Slow Mountain Train, by Roger Greenwald
The Burning Door, by Tony Leuzzi
I've Come This Far to Say Hello: Poems Selected and New, by Kurt Brown
After That, by Kathleen Aguero
Crossing the Yellow River, trans. Sam Hamill
Night Garden, by Judith Harris
Time~Bound, by Kurt Brown
Sweet Weight, by Kate Lynn Hibbard
The Gate at Visby, by Deena Linett
River of Glass, by Ann McGovern
Inside Such Darkness, by Virginia Slachman
Transfiguration Begins at Home, by Estha Weiner
The Solvay Process, by Martin Walls
A Pilgrim into Silence, by Karen Swenson